100 DAYS
of PRAYER

 FriesenPress

One Printers Way
Altona, MB R0G 0B0
Canada

www.friesenpress.com

Author's Photograph by Christina Esteban

ISBN
978-1-03-914522-1 (Hardcover)
978-1-03-914521-4 (Paperback)
978-1-03-914523-8 (eBook)

1. RELIGION, CHRISTIAN LIFE, PRAYER

Distributed to the trade by The Ingram Book Company

100 DAYS
of PRAYER

———

a journey into deeper intimacy with God

ruth hovsepian

For my parents, Joseph (Hovsep) and Jessie (Hasmig), who
love me unconditionally and pray for me daily.

For my sister, Ann-Margret, who without her foresight and
encouragement this book would not have been possible.

For my three children, Alexis, Joshua, and Melissa, who inspire me
and make me so proud. Always look to the Lord for guidance.

For my angel in heaven, my first-born granddaughter,
Eloise Monroe—a moment in our arms, a lifetime in our hearts.

Evening, morning and noon
I cry out in distress,
and he hears my voice.

PSALM 55:17

BOOK BELONGS TO

_____

Pray

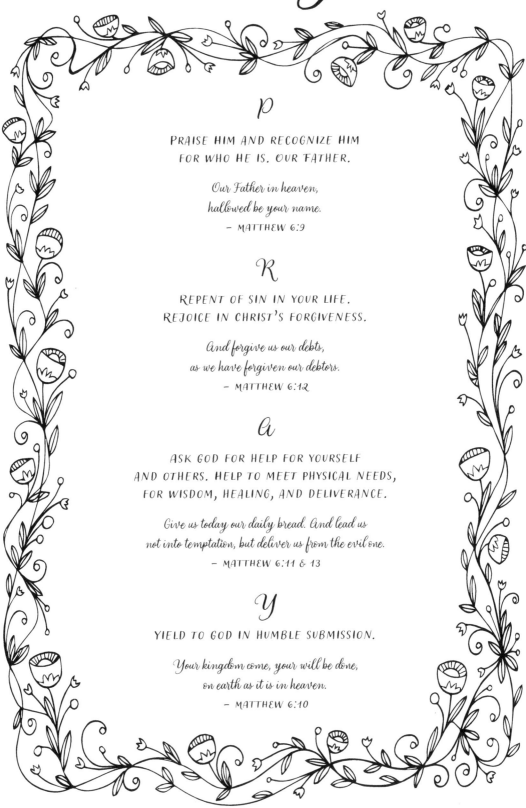

P

PRAISE HIM AND RECOGNIZE HIM
FOR WHO HE IS, OUR FATHER.

Our Father in heaven,
hallowed be your name.
— MATTHEW 6:9

R

REPENT OF SIN IN YOUR LIFE.
REJOICE IN CHRIST'S FORGIVENESS.

And forgive us our debts,
as we have forgiven our debtors.
— MATTHEW 6:12

A

ASK GOD FOR HELP FOR YOURSELF
AND OTHERS. HELP TO MEET PHYSICAL NEEDS,
FOR WISDOM, HEALING, AND DELIVERANCE.

Give us today our daily bread. And lead us
not into temptation, but deliver us from the evil one.
— MATTHEW 6:11 & 13

Y

YIELD TO GOD IN HUMBLE SUBMISSION.

Your kingdom come, your will be done,
on earth as it is in heaven.
— MATTHEW 6:10

Contents

A journey into deeper intimacy with God

Do you ever wonder how effective your prayer life is? Perhaps you wonder: *Do I need to pray? Does God even hear me? Does He care? Am I praying the right way? Am I praying enough?*

We've all been there. I certainly have, even though I learned to pray as early as I learned to talk. I still remember the Armenian prayer I was taught as a child that I prayed until my early twenties. It was said before meals and went something like this:

> *Ov der, orhne mer seghane* (O Lord, bless our table)
> *Vorbesi mer geragournere* (so that our food)
> *Mezi zoroutchyoun dalov* (giving us strength)
> *Ku gamked gadarenq.* (we may do your will.)
> *Axkatnerouna dour, Hisous.* (And give to the poor, Jesus.)
> *Amen*

I can still recite this prayer in my sleep. As I got older and understood prayer should be more than just a recited one, I tried slowing myself down as I said this childhood prayer but, after a while, I knew this prayer was no longer fitting for giving thanks. Even though I no longer recite this childhood prayer, I frequently pray in my mother tongue, Armenian.

Growing up in an evangelical family, I heard the word "prayer" often. If someone had to make a decision, they were encouraged to pray. If someone was sick, they were told to pray about their illness. Prayer was the answer if someone was struggling with life, family, children, work, or any other problem. Well, not exactly the answer, but the way to *get* a response or God's help resolving an issue.

My paternal grandmother spent hours praying—quietly on her own, with my grandfather, or on the phone with others. She prayed so much on the phone that the family installed a second line to keep the first one available for emergencies. When the "red phone" rang while we were visiting, we knew the incoming call was for prayer. No nonsensical conversation on the red phone. Straight to prayer!

Examples of answered prayers surrounded me and, although some prayers were for and about me, I never took that as a reason to develop a prayer life of my own. Like most people, prayer was how I communicated my difficulties and requests to God. Not much thought and time went into it.

As a child, I would pray on my knees by my bed before bed. If I forgot to, I'd jump out of bed feeling guilty and fearful that God would strike me dead or, worse, send me to hell. Over time, this habit and fear wore off.

In my 30s and 40s, when I went through later-in-life turmoil and rebellion, there was no way I could pray. That would involve "showing" God my dirty insides. How could I pray and speak to God when my life was full of filth and sin? Praying was too intimate. It made me feel vulnerable. Praying would shine a light on my wrongdoings.

The farther from God I moved, the colder my prayer line became. I wandered so far away that I silenced any guilt I felt as a child when I didn't pray.

By the world's standards, I was on top of the world. With only trade school training, I had landed a high-level corporate position bringing in six figures with five-figure bonuses. I had a busy social life, never paid for drinks or meals, and got into clubs and private parties without waiting in line. I had so many dates I lost track of names and faces. It was a fast-paced life. I worked hard and played even harder.

I took a path trod by many, which led to self-destruction, a path that would ultimately lead to one destination only: the belly of hell. The farther along this path I walked, the lonelier I felt. The noise in my head and around me got louder, and I could not silence it.

There was a price to pay for my lifestyle: *loneliness*.

At the highest point in my career, God kicked my feet right out from under me.

CRASH.

I fell far and hard.

My pride was hurt.

I didn't know who to turn to.

I hid.

I hid from the world, family, and GOD.

What now?

I struggled, ignoring what was lurking in the shadows.

"Come to me, all you who are weary and burdened, and I will give you rest" (Matthew 11:28).

IGNORE.

"Do not fear, for I am with you" (Isaiah 41:10).

BE QUIET.

Verses I had read and memorized in my childhood began to haunt me.

Stumbling home early one morning after partying all night, I crawled into bed. Alone. So alone, it hurt. It hurt more than any physical pain I had ever experienced.

There was a pain in my heart that nothing seemed to relieve. That was the beginning of my journey. It wasn't a journey without detours and bumps and struggles. It took years of two steps forward and one step back—years of denying the offered hand that God extended to me.

The thing that affected and aligned me was when I started to pray, or at least tried to, my first attempts were childlike. Hesitant. I struggled to find words. I wasn't ready to admit my mistakes, struggles, needs, and weaknesses to anyone including God.

One prayer at a time. One day at a time. That's how I turned my life around. With each prayer, the words came easier. I no longer hesitated to speak with the Lord about what was weighing on my heart or what I was struggling with.

As my heart and life were righted, I slowly realized I was only *asking* for things and not *thanking* God for all He was doing in my life. I knew I needed to start acknowledging and thanking Him for His blessings. It became my goal to become more intentional about my prayer life.

The first change I made was writing down a list of names of people I wanted to pray for. The list helped me focus on others, think less about myself, and avoid the *me-me-me* syndrome. I also began to write down answers to prayers and blessings and note things I was grateful about.

One day, after I got off the phone, I realized that the person had asked for prayer for a very specific need, and I almost forgot my promise to pray for them. I had an aha moment and knew that if I didn't start a list of prayer requests, I would never be able to keep my word. This practice helped me become diligent about praying for specific needs and requests. The format of my lists evolved over time and eventually led to the creation of *100 Days of Prayer*.

Why 100 Days of Prayer?

Prayer is an intimate journey with God into intimacy with God. It isn't a means to an end, but, instead, it is itself a gift to be treasured and enjoyed. Too often, we use prayer to GET THINGS from God. Instead, we should use prayer to GET GOD, to simply bask in His presence, adore Him, learn from Him, find our strength in Him, and be reminded of His love for us.

This book invites you to commit the next 100 days to develop the beautiful discipline of being still and intentional about prayer. In the pages ahead, you will find scripture inspiration to help you better understand prayer, as well as a process for organizing and keeping track of prayer requests. You'll be prompted to reflect on daily blessings, goals, and insights.

Prayer is important because it's how...

... we communicate with God.
"When you call out to me and come to me in prayer, I will hear your prayers" (Jeremiah 29:12 NET).

... we express our gratitude.
"I will give thanks to you, LORD, with all my heart; I will tell of all your wonderful deeds" (Psalm 9:1 NIV).

... we praise God.
"Enter his gates with thanksgiving, and his courts with praise! Give thanks to him; bless his name! For the LORD is good; his steadfast love endures forever, and his faithfulness to all generations" (Psalm 100:4–5 ESV).

... we ask for help.
"Ask and it will be given to you; seek, and you will find; knock, and the door will be opened to you" (Matthew 7:7 ESV).

... we ask for what we need.
"Do not be anxious about anything, but in every situation, by prayer and petition, with thanksgiving, present your requests to God" (Philippians 4:6 NIV).

... we confess our sins.
"If we confess our sins, he is faithful and just to forgive us our sins and to cleanse us from all unrighteousness" (1 John 1:9 ESV).

... we receive salvation.
"And it shall come to pass that everyone who calls upon the name of the Lord shall be saved" (Acts 2:21 ESV).

... we intercede for others.
"First of all, then, I urge that requests, prayers, intercessions, and thanks be offered on behalf of all people" (1 Timothy 2:1 NET).

... we resist temptation.
"Watch and pray so that you will not fall into temptation. The spirit is willing, but the flesh is weak" (Matthew 26:41 NIV).

... we bless our enemies.
"But I say to you who hear, Love your enemies, do good to those who hate you, bless those who curse you, pray for those who abuse you" (Luke 6:27–28 ESV).

How to Use This Book

100 Days of Prayer brings together biblical guidelines, real-life examples (mine!), and practical templates to help you record your general prayer lists as well as your specific requests, personal reflections, praise items, and answers to prayer.

I invite you to journey with me as I share my heart and tell you about the circuitous journey my prayer life has taken—the peaks and valleys that eventually led me to a place of quiet understanding. My experiences have helped me develop a mindful, ordered, and enriching prayer life.

My goal is to help you move past the desert of seeing prayer as a mere duty to check off your daily to-do list and come into the green pastures of precious communion with God; to rise above the guilt we all experience when we forget to pray after promising and to find joy in lifting those needs God puts on your heart; and, finally, to take time to truly acknowledge specific blessings and answered prayers.

The first journaling section provides a place for you to list names for daily prayer and note specific needs for each one, followed by a place to list names for occasional prayer (friends, people in the community, ministries and people in ministry, and others).

Then we start the 100-day journey, divided into ten chapters; each chapter focuses on one of the reasons praying is important (which we covered on the previous page). Each ten-day chapter starts with a theme verse, a short reflection from my own life, a suggested prayer, a hymn to meditate on (with an accompanying illustrated page you can color in), and then ten daily journaling pages with prompts to respond to, inviting you to record gratitude lists, needs, aspirations, evening reflections, and other notes.

At the back of the book, you'll find a chart to log prayer requests received, with space to record the name, date, area of need, timeline, follow-up dates, and the outcome.

Prayer List

NAMES FOR DAILY PRAYER

NAME
_____

PRAYER REQUESTS
_____
_____
_____
_____
_____

NAME
_____

PRAYER REQUESTS
_____
_____
_____
_____
_____

NAME
_____

PRAYER REQUESTS
_____
_____
_____
_____
_____

NAME
_____

PRAYER REQUESTS
_____
_____
_____
_____
_____

NAME

PRAYER REQUESTS

NAME

PRAYER REQUESTS

NAME

PRAYER REQUESTS

NAME

PRAYER REQUESTS

Hear my voice when I call, Lord; Be merciful to me an answer me. – Psalm 27:7

Prayer List

NAMES FOR OCCASIONAL PRAYER

FRIENDS & FAMILY

PEOPLE IN THE COMMUNITY

MINISTRIES & PEOPLE IN MINISTRY

OTHER PEOPLE

Therefore confess your sins to each other and pray for each other so that you may be healed. The prayer of a righteous person is powerful and effective. – James 5:16

DAYS 1 TO 10:

Prayer Is How
We Communicate with God

When you call out to me and come to me in prayer,
I will hear your prayers. – Jeremiah 29:12

When I look back at my marriage, I realize that we had stopped communicating with each other. We were living together but walking down different paths. Perhaps if we had told each other what was in our hearts, our marriage vows would have held up.

Any relationship without communication will not move forward. A dating couple who never communicates cannot expect the relationship to move ahead. A married couple who no longer talk ends up wondering how they drifted so far apart. The same is true when we have drifted away from God's presence because we no longer communicate with Him.

Satan wants to distract us in any way possible. That's why Peter wrote, "Be sober-minded; be watchful. Your adversary the devil prowls around like a roaring lion, seeking someone to devour" (1 Peter 5:8). The best way to counteract this is to "submit yourselves therefore to God. Resist the devil, and he will flee from you" (James 4:7).

God hears, and He answers well.

God tells us to pray and call out to Him. When we do this with our whole heart, He will rescue and restore us.

When we are going through difficulties or circumstances beyond our understanding, we must pray to God and rely on Him.

Our world has become so consumed with careers, worldly pleasures, and technology that the only time we may speak with God is right before we go to sleep with a quick prayer. Or when things are going horribly wrong, we question God angrily.

We must walk with the Lord and draw closer to Him; this will make Him the focus of our lives. As we seek His presence, the more our heart longs for Him. The more we fellowship with Him and want to be like Him, our worldly desires will diminish.

Lord, every day I call on You. Every day I pray and listen and watch for your answer. I believe that you hear me and will respond. Help me to recognize when and how you are responding. I long for your presence in my life, Lord, and I know you are willing and able to do that. In Jesus' name, Amen.

I NEED THEE EVERY HOUR
by Annie Sherwood Hawks

I need Thee every hour,
Most gracious Lord
No tender voice like Thine
Can peace afford

Chorus
I need Thee, O I need Thee,
Every hour I need Thee!
O bless me now, my Savior,
I come to Thee!

I need Thee every hour,
Stay Thou near by;
Temptations lose their power
When Thou art nigh. (chorus)

I need Thee every hour,
In joy, or pain;
Come quickly and abide
Or life is vain. (chorus)

I need Thee every hour,
Teach me Thy will;
Thy promises so rich
In me fulfill. (chorus)

I need Thee every hour,
Most Holy One,
O make me Thine indeed,
Thou Blessed Son! (chorus)

Daily Prayers

DATE _____

I'M GRATEFUL FOR:

_____
_____
_____
_____
_____
_____
_____
_____
_____
_____

TODAY I NEED:

_____
_____
_____
_____

TODAY I ASPIRE TO:

_____
_____
_____
_____
_____

○◉○◉○◉○◉○◉○

Evening Reflections

TODAY I LEARNED:

_____

TODAY I WAS CHALLENGED BY:

_____

TODAY I WAS HAPPY THAT:

_____

Prayer Tip - Create A Prayer Spot

IT DOESN'T REALLY MATTER WHERE YOU PRAY TO GOD, IT WILL HELP YOU PREPARE YOUR MIND FOR
PRAYER. FIND A QUIET SPOT IN YOUR HOME, EVEN A CLOSET WILL DO. DOING THIS WILL HELP YOU FOCUS
AND BE CONSISTENT WITH YOUR PRAYER TIME.

DATE _____

Daily Prayers

I'M GRATEFUL FOR:

_____
_____
_____
_____
_____
_____
_____
_____
_____
_____
_____

TODAY I NEED:

_____
_____
_____
_____

TODAY I ASPIRE TO:

_____
_____
_____
_____

Evening Reflections

TODAY I LEARNED:

_____
_____

TODAY I WAS CHALLENGED BY:

_____
_____

TODAY I WAS HAPPY THAT:

_____
_____

DATE _____

Daily Prayers

I'M GRATEFUL FOR:

_____
_____
_____
_____
_____
_____
_____
_____
_____
_____

TODAY I NEED:

_____
_____
_____
_____

TODAY I ASPIRE TO:

_____
_____
_____
_____
_____

Evening Reflections

TODAY I LEARNED:

_____

TODAY I WAS CHALLENGED BY:

_____
_____

TODAY I WAS HAPPY THAT:

_____

DATE _____

Daily Prayers

I'M GRATEFUL FOR:

_____
_____
_____
_____
_____
_____
_____
_____
_____
_____
_____

TODAY I NEED:

_____
_____
_____
_____

TODAY I ASPIRE TO:

_____
_____
_____
_____
_____

Evening Reflections

TODAY I LEARNED:

_____
_____

TODAY I WAS CHALLENGED BY:

_____
_____

TODAY I WAS HAPPY THAT:

_____
_____

DATE _____

Daily Prayers

I'M GRATEFUL FOR:

_____
_____
_____
_____
_____
_____
_____
_____
_____
_____

TODAY I NEED:

_____
_____
_____
_____

TODAY I ASPIRE TO:

_____
_____
_____
_____

∘◉∘◉∘◉∘◉∘◉∘

Evening Reflections

TODAY I LEARNED:

_____
_____

TODAY I WAS CHALLENGED BY:

_____
_____

TODAY I WAS HAPPY THAT:

_____
_____

DATE _____

Daily Prayers

I'M GRATEFUL FOR:

_____
_____
_____
_____
_____
_____
_____
_____
_____

TODAY I NEED:

_____
_____
_____
_____

TODAY I ASPIRE TO:

_____
_____
_____
_____

Evening Reflections

TODAY I LEARNED:

_____

TODAY I WAS CHALLENGED BY:

_____

TODAY I WAS HAPPY THAT:

_____

Quote of the Day
"OUR PRAYERS MAY BE AWKWARD. OUR ATTEMPTS MAY BE FEEBLE. BUT SINCE THE POWER OF PRAYER IS IN THE ONE WHO HEARS IT AND NOT IN THE ONE WHO SAYS IT, OUR PRAYERS DO MAKE A DIFFERENCE." — MAX LUCADO

DATE _____

Daily Prayers

I'M GRATEFUL FOR:

_____
_____
_____
_____
_____
_____
_____
_____
_____
_____

TODAY I NEED:

_____
_____
_____
_____

TODAY I ASPIRE TO:

_____
_____
_____
_____
_____

Evening Reflections

TODAY I LEARNED:

_____
_____

TODAY I WAS CHALLENGED BY:

_____
_____

TODAY I WAS HAPPY THAT:

_____
_____

DATE _____

Daily Prayers

I'M GRATEFUL FOR:

_____
_____
_____
_____
_____
_____
_____
_____
_____
_____
_____
_____

TODAY I NEED:

_____
_____
_____
_____
_____

TODAY I ASPIRE TO:

_____
_____
_____
_____
_____

Evening Reflections

TODAY I LEARNED:

_____
_____

TODAY I WAS CHALLENGED BY:

_____
_____

TODAY I WAS HAPPY THAT:

_____

DATE _____

Daily Prayers

I'M GRATEFUL FOR:

_____
_____
_____
_____
_____
_____
_____
_____
_____
_____
_____

TODAY I NEED:

_____
_____
_____
_____

TODAY I ASPIRE TO:

_____
_____
_____
_____
_____
_____

◦ ❀ ◦ ❀ ◦ ❀ ◦ ❀ ◦ ❀ ◦

Evening Reflections

TODAY I LEARNED:

_____
_____

TODAY I WAS CHALLENGED BY:

_____
_____

TODAY I WAS HAPPY THAT:

_____
_____

DATE _____

Daily Prayers

I'M GRATEFUL FOR:

_____
_____
_____
_____
_____
_____
_____
_____
_____
_____
_____

TODAY I NEED:

_____
_____
_____
_____

TODAY I ASPIRE TO:

_____
_____
_____
_____
_____

Evening Reflections

TODAY I LEARNED:

_____
_____

TODAY I WAS CHALLENGED BY:

_____
_____

TODAY I WAS HAPPY THAT:

_____
_____

DAYS 11 TO 20:

Prayer Is How
We Express Our Gratitude

I will give thanks to you, LORD, with all my heart;
I will tell of all your wonderful deeds. – Psalm 9:1

This verse reminds us to give thanks and transform our hearts into grateful hearts. To open our eyes to all the wonderful works and deeds that God has done for us. This verse is a reminder of God's love and faithfulness.

David is teaching us to respond with thanksgiving and praise during hardships in our life. When we suffer, our focus tends to shrink to a point where only our circumstances are visible.

Gratitude glorifies God. This alone should be reason enough for us to give thanks to God. Our gratitude is not only for the things we have received but for the One who has given us these gifts. Through this, I have learned to be intentional about telling others of God's glory. When we proclaim all that, He has done, we declare to the world that we have a caring and personal God.

A great exercise that has worked for me has been to count my blessings. Counting my blessings and being grateful for them has helped me see that God's hand is all over my life. And God tells us when we give Him our thanks, He gives us supernatural peace.

With this came contentment and joy in a way that I had not experienced before. I learned that if I weren't grateful for what I had, I would never be happy no matter what else came into my life.

With gratitude comes a deeper faith and a closer relationship with God. When we realize how undeserving we are of His kindness, we draw closer to Him.

Having a grateful heart is the beginning of many blessings.

Lord, I thank you for all your blessings in my life.
Help me remember just how blessed I am and show my gratitude in
prayer and in returned acts of kindness. Thank you, Lord. Amen.

Come, Thou Fount of Every Blessing
by Robert Robinson

Come Thou Fount of every blessing
Tune my heart to sing Thy grace;
Streams of mercy, never ceasing,
Call for songs of loudest praise
Teach me some melodious sonnet,
Sung by flaming tongues above.
Praise the mount! I'm fixed upon it,
Mount of God's unchanging love.

Here I raise my Ebenezer;
Hither by Thy help I'm come;
And I hope, by Thy good pleasure,
Safely to arrive at home.
Jesus sought me when a stranger,
Wandering from the fold of God;
He, to rescue me from danger,
Interposed His precious blood.

O to grace how great a debtor
Daily I'm constrained to be!
Let that grace now like a fetter,
Bind my wandering heart to Thee.
Prone to wander, Lord, I feel it,
Prone to leave the God I love;
Here's my heart, O take and seal it,
Seal it for Thy courts above.

DATE _____

Daily Prayers

I'M GRATEFUL FOR:

_____
_____
_____
_____
_____
_____
_____
_____
_____
_____
_____

TODAY I NEED:

_____
_____
_____
_____

TODAY I ASPIRE TO:

_____
_____
_____
_____
_____
_____

Evening Reflections

TODAY I LEARNED:

_____

TODAY I WAS CHALLENGED BY:

_____

TODAY I WAS HAPPY THAT:

_____

Prayer Tip – Schedule Prayer Time

WHEN FIRST STARTING OUT, A FEW MINUTES WILL BE ALL YOU WILL BE ABLE TO DO. BUT AS YOU ARE CONSISTENT WITH YOUR DAILY PRAYER TIME, YOU WILL NOTICE THAT YOUR TIME WILL ALSO GROW. SCHEDULING PRAYER TIME DOES NOT MEAN YOU DO NOT PRAY OUTSIDE OF THIS TIME; WE SHOULD BE IN CONTINUAL PRAYER THROUGHOUT OUR DAY (1 THESSALONIANS 5:17). IT DOES MEAN THAT YOU ARE PUTTING ASIDE TIME TO FOCUS ON THE LORD.

Daily Prayers

I'M GRATEFUL FOR:

_____
_____
_____
_____
_____
_____
_____
_____
_____
_____
_____

TODAY I NEED:

_____
_____
_____
_____

TODAY I ASPIRE TO:

_____
_____
_____
_____
_____

Evening Reflections

TODAY I LEARNED:

_____
_____

TODAY I WAS CHALLENGED BY:

_____
_____

TODAY I WAS HAPPY THAT:

_____
_____

Daily Prayers

DATE_____

I'M GRATEFUL FOR:

_____
_____
_____
_____
_____
_____
_____
_____
_____
_____
_____

TODAY I NEED:

_____
_____
_____
_____

TODAY I ASPIRE TO:

_____
_____
_____
_____
_____
_____

○◉○◉○◉○◉○◉○

Evening Reflections

TODAY I LEARNED:

_____
_____

TODAY I WAS CHALLENGED BY:

_____
_____

TODAY I WAS HAPPY THAT:

_____
_____

Daily Prayers

I'M GRATEFUL FOR:

_____
_____
_____
_____
_____
_____
_____
_____
_____
_____
_____

TODAY I NEED:

_____
_____
_____
_____

TODAY I ASPIRE TO:

_____
_____
_____
_____
_____

Evening Reflections

TODAY I LEARNED:

_____
_____

TODAY I WAS CHALLENGED BY:

_____
_____

TODAY I WAS HAPPY THAT:

_____
_____

DATE _____

Daily Prayers

I'M GRATEFUL FOR:

_____
_____
_____
_____
_____
_____
_____
_____
_____
_____
_____

TODAY I NEED:

_____
_____
_____
_____
_____

TODAY I ASPIRE TO:

_____
_____
_____
_____
_____

Evening Reflections

TODAY I LEARNED:

_____
_____

TODAY I WAS CHALLENGED BY:

_____
_____

TODAY I WAS HAPPY THAT:

_____

DATE _____

Daily Prayers

I'M GRATEFUL FOR:

_____
_____
_____
_____
_____
_____
_____
_____
_____
_____
_____

TODAY I NEED:

_____
_____
_____
_____

TODAY I ASPIRE TO:

_____
_____
_____
_____
_____

Evening Reflections

TODAY I LEARNED:

_____

TODAY I WAS CHALLENGED BY:

_____

TODAY I WAS HAPPY THAT:

_____

Quote of the Day

"TO BE A CHRISTIAN WITHOUT PRAYER IS NO MORE POSSIBLE THAN
TO BE ALIVE WITHOUT BREATHING." — MARTIN LUTHER

DATE _____

Daily Prayers

I'M GRATEFUL FOR:

_____

_____

_____

_____

_____

_____

_____

_____

_____

TODAY I NEED:

_____

_____

_____

_____

TODAY I ASPIRE TO:

_____

_____

_____

_____

_____

Evening Reflections

TODAY I LEARNED:

_____

_____

TODAY I WAS CHALLENGED BY:

_____

_____

TODAY I WAS HAPPY THAT:

_____

DATE _____

Daily Prayers

I'M GRATEFUL FOR:

_____
_____
_____
_____
_____
_____
_____
_____
_____

TODAY I NEED:

_____
_____
_____

TODAY I ASPIRE TO:

_____
_____
_____
_____
_____

Evening Reflections

TODAY I LEARNED:

_____
_____

TODAY I WAS CHALLENGED BY:

_____
_____

TODAY I WAS HAPPY THAT:

_____
_____

DATE _____

Daily Prayers

I'M GRATEFUL FOR:

_____
_____
_____
_____
_____
_____
_____
_____
_____
_____

TODAY I NEED:

_____
_____
_____
_____

TODAY I ASPIRE TO:

_____
_____
_____
_____

Evening Reflections

TODAY I LEARNED:

_____
_____

TODAY I WAS CHALLENGED BY:

_____
_____

TODAY I WAS HAPPY THAT:

_____
_____

DATE _____

Daily Prayers

I'M GRATEFUL FOR:

_____
_____
_____
_____
_____
_____
_____
_____
_____
_____

TODAY I NEED:

_____
_____
_____
_____

TODAY I ASPIRE TO:

_____
_____
_____
_____
_____

Evening Reflections

TODAY I LEARNED:

_____
_____

TODAY I WAS CHALLENGED BY:

_____
_____

TODAY I WAS HAPPY THAT:

_____
_____

DAYS 21 TO 30:

Prayer Is How
We Praise God

Enter his gates with thanksgiving, and his courts with praise! Give thanks to him; bless his name! For the Lord is good; his steadfast love endures forever, and his faithfulness to all generations. — Psalm 100:4–5

We all go through pain or loss in our lives. During those difficult times, it is normal to feel sadness and depression. Praising God during these times builds a shield to protect our hearts and minds so that we do not sink deep into despair. Praise drives away depression and brings victory.

In a world focused on "selfies," we need to look around and remember that life is not only about us. Human nature is such that we sometimes let our hearts think for us and forget what we know. We are born selfish. God's desire for us is to set our eyes firmly on Him. Our hope is rooted in the Lord. He is worthy of our praise. No matter what we come face to face with daily, He is worthy of our praise. Praise satisfies our souls.

Several years ago, I decided to start my days by beginning my prayers with praise and thanksgiving for all the things and people in my life. Starting my prayers with praise and thanksgiving makes God's presence closer, and I feel comforted, and I can deal with what life has in store for me in a much more positive attitude.

Adding praise changed the way I pray because I started to see God differently, which made my relationship with Him closer. Praise shifted the focus off of me and on to God. Praise invites God's presence into our lives.

How do we cultivate a life of praise during everyday ups and downs?

When fears and worries are overwhelming you, stop, breathe, and praise God. Overcome fear and worry with praise.

Praise strengthens us.

Dear Heavenly Father, thank you that your mercy endures forever. I thank you for sending Jesus, who died and shed His precious blood on the cross, that I might live in a relationship with you forever. Amen.

Thee will
I cherish,
Thee will
I honor.

Fairest Lord Jesus
by Joseph Seiss

Beautiful Savior, King of Creation
Son of God and Son of Man!
Truly I'd love Thee, truly I'd serve Thee,
Light of my soul, my joy, my crown.

Fair are the meadows, Fair are the woodlands,
Robed in the flowers of blooming spring;
Jesus is fairer, Jesus is purer,
He makes our sorrowing spirit sing.

Fair is the sunshine, Fair is the moonlight,
Bright the sparkling stars on high;
Jesus shines brighter, Jesus shines purer
Than all the angels in the sky.

Daily Prayers

I'M GRATEFUL FOR:

_____
_____
_____
_____
_____
_____
_____
_____
_____
_____

TODAY I NEED:

_____
_____
_____
_____

TODAY I ASPIRE TO:

_____
_____
_____
_____
_____
_____

Evening Reflections

TODAY I LEARNED:

_____

TODAY I WAS CHALLENGED BY:

_____

TODAY I WAS HAPPY THAT:

_____

Prayer Tip – Start With Just One

WHEN I STARTED TO PRAY, I STARTED WITH ONE REQUEST AT A TIME. IT CAN SOMETIMES BE OVERWHELMING,
AND WE STRUGGLE FOR WORDS. I NOW PRAY FOR MANY, BUT IT ALL STARTED FROM "JUST ONE."

DATE _____

Daily Prayers

I'M GRATEFUL FOR:

_____
_____
_____
_____
_____
_____
_____
_____
_____
_____
_____

TODAY I NEED:

_____
_____
_____
_____
_____

TODAY I ASPIRE TO:

_____
_____
_____
_____
_____

Evening Reflections

TODAY I LEARNED:

_____
_____

TODAY I WAS CHALLENGED BY:

_____
_____

TODAY I WAS HAPPY THAT:

_____

DATE _____

Daily Prayers

I'M GRATEFUL FOR:

_____
_____
_____
_____
_____
_____
_____
_____
_____

TODAY I NEED:

_____
_____
_____
_____

TODAY I ASPIRE TO:

_____
_____
_____
_____

○◉○◉○◉○◉○◉○◉○

Evening Reflections

TODAY I LEARNED:

_____
_____

TODAY I WAS CHALLENGED BY:

_____
_____

TODAY I WAS HAPPY THAT:

_____
_____

DATE _____

Daily Prayers

I'M GRATEFUL FOR:

_____
_____
_____
_____
_____
_____
_____
_____
_____
_____

TODAY I NEED:

_____
_____
_____
_____

TODAY I ASPIRE TO:

_____
_____
_____
_____

Evening Reflections

TODAY I LEARNED:

_____
_____

TODAY I WAS CHALLENGED BY:

_____
_____

TODAY I WAS HAPPY THAT:

_____
_____

DATE _____

Daily Prayers

I'M GRATEFUL FOR:

_____
_____
_____
_____
_____
_____
_____
_____
_____

TODAY I NEED:

_____
_____
_____
_____

TODAY I ASPIRE TO:

_____
_____
_____
_____

Evening Reflections

TODAY I LEARNED:

_____
_____

TODAY I WAS CHALLENGED BY:

_____
_____

TODAY I WAS HAPPY THAT:

_____
_____

DATE _____

Daily Prayers

I'M GRATEFUL FOR:

_____
_____
_____
_____
_____
_____
_____
_____
_____
_____

TODAY I NEED:

_____
_____
_____
_____

TODAY I ASPIRE TO:

_____
_____
_____
_____

○○◉○◉○◉○◉○

Evening Reflections

TODAY I LEARNED:

_____

TODAY I WAS CHALLENGED BY:

_____

TODAY I WAS HAPPY THAT:

_____

Quote of the Day

"IF YOU BELIEVE IN PRAYER AT ALL, EXPECT GOD TO HEAR YOU. IF YOU DO NOT EXPECT, YOU WILL NOT HAVE. GOD WILL NOT HEAR YOU UNLESS YOU BELIEVE HE WILL HEAR YOU; BUT IF YOU BELIEVE HE WILL, HE WILL BE AS GOOD AS YOUR FAITH." — CHARLES SPURGEON

DATE _____

Daily Prayers

I'M GRATEFUL FOR:

_____
_____
_____
_____
_____
_____
_____
_____
_____

TODAY I NEED:

_____
_____
_____
_____
_____

TODAY I ASPIRE TO:

_____
_____
_____
_____
_____

Evening Reflections

TODAY I LEARNED:

_____
_____

TODAY I WAS CHALLENGED BY:

_____
_____

TODAY I WAS HAPPY THAT:

_____

DATE _____

Daily Prayers

I'M GRATEFUL FOR:

_____
_____
_____
_____
_____
_____
_____
_____
_____
_____
_____
_____
_____

TODAY I NEED:

_____
_____
_____
_____

TODAY I ASPIRE TO:

_____
_____
_____
_____
_____

Evening Reflections

TODAY I LEARNED:

_____

TODAY I WAS CHALLENGED BY:

_____
_____

TODAY I WAS HAPPY THAT:

_____

DATE _____

Daily Prayers

I'M GRATEFUL FOR:

_____
_____
_____
_____
_____
_____
_____
_____
_____
_____
_____
_____

TODAY I NEED:

_____
_____
_____
_____

TODAY I ASPIRE TO:

_____
_____
_____
_____
_____

Evening Reflections

TODAY I LEARNED:

_____
_____

TODAY I WAS CHALLENGED BY:

_____
_____

TODAY I WAS HAPPY THAT:

_____
_____

Daily Prayers

I'M GRATEFUL FOR:

_____
_____
_____
_____
_____
_____
_____
_____
_____
_____

TODAY I NEED:

_____
_____
_____
_____

TODAY I ASPIRE TO:

_____
_____
_____
_____

Evening Reflections

TODAY I LEARNED:

_____
_____

TODAY I WAS CHALLENGED BY:

_____
_____

TODAY I WAS HAPPY THAT:

_____
_____

DAYS 31 TO 40:

Prayer Is How We Ask for Help

Ask and it will be given to you; seek and you will find;
knock, and the door will be opened to you. – Matthew 7:7

Pornography hooked me and then reeled me in. Like any other addiction, I needed porn more often to keep those same good feelings. Shame and disgust were eternal companions, but I was driven to watch more and more frequently. The call of sexual sin was strong. I was addicted to the feeling.

20% of all Christian women are addicted to pornography.

"'More than 80 percent of women who have this addiction take it offline,' says Marnie Ferree. 'Women, far more than men, are likely to act out their behaviors in real life, such as having multiple partners, casual sex, or affairs.'"[i]

When I gave my life to the Lord, I could no longer keep this behavior going. I confessed to my secret addiction. "I know I should pray when I am tempted, but I am so embarrassed to bring this to God. I feel so dirty." Through Christ's love, patience and forgiveness, I learned to redirect my thoughts to God when temptation reared its ugly head.

I know that I am not alone in this struggle. I want to share Hebrews 4:15 with you, "We do not have a high priest who is unable to empathize with our weaknesses, but we have one who has been tempted in every way, just as we are—yet he did not sin."

When the Israelites sinned against God, they would bring Him a sacrifice. The high priest would do the messy job of killing the animal. Then, the high priest would bring it to God as an atonement for their sins. When Jesus died on the Cross, He became the High Priest. The devil tempted Jesus to sin. He was tempted to sin "in every way."

There may not have been the internet or cell phones, but sexual sin isn't a new temptation; sexual temptations have been around for a very long time.

When you face temptation, take it to Jesus. Lay it at is feet. Be open and honest about your struggles and temptations. Don't deal with it alone.

Jesus, help me in my time of need.
I am tempted to sin; please set me free!
I want to live my life in a way that it will honor You.
In Your name, Amen.

Spirit of God, descend upon my heart;

Spirit of God, Descend Upon My Heart
by George Croly

Spirit of God, descend upon my heart;
Wean it from earth; through all its pulses move;
Stoop to my weakness, mighty as Thou art;
And make me love Thee as I ought to love.

I ask no dream, no prophet ecstasies,
No sudden rending of the veil of clay,
No angel visitant, no opening skies;
But take the dimness of my soul away.

Teach me to feel that Thou art always nigh;
Teach me the struggles of the soul to bear.
To check the rising doubt, the rebel sigh,
Teach me the patience of unanswered prayer.

DATE _____

Daily Prayers

I'M GRATEFUL FOR:

_____
_____
_____
_____
_____
_____
_____
_____
_____
_____

TODAY I NEED:

_____
_____
_____
_____

TODAY I ASPIRE TO:

_____
_____
_____
_____
_____

Evening Reflections

TODAY I LEARNED:

_____

TODAY I WAS CHALLENGED BY:

_____

TODAY I WAS HAPPY THAT:

_____

Prayer Tip – Create a Prayer List

KEEP A LIST OF YOUR OWN NEEDS, THOSE OF YOUR FAMILY AND
FRIENDS, AND ANY REQUESTS THAT THEY MAY TELL YOU.

DATE _____

Daily Prayers

I'M GRATEFUL FOR:

_____
_____
_____
_____
_____
_____
_____
_____
_____
_____
_____

TODAY I NEED:

_____
_____
_____

TODAY I ASPIRE TO:

_____
_____
_____
_____

Evening Reflections

TODAY I LEARNED:

_____
_____

TODAY I WAS CHALLENGED BY:

_____
_____

TODAY I WAS HAPPY THAT:

_____

DATE_____

Daily Prayers

I'M GRATEFUL FOR:

_____
_____
_____
_____
_____
_____
_____
_____
_____
_____

TODAY I NEED:

_____
_____
_____

TODAY I ASPIRE TO:

_____
_____
_____
_____
_____

∘❀∘❀∘❀∘❀∘❀∘

Evening Reflections

TODAY I LEARNED:

_____
_____

TODAY I WAS CHALLENGED BY:

_____
_____

TODAY I WAS HAPPY THAT:

_____
_____

DATE _____

Daily Prayers

I'M GRATEFUL FOR:

_____
_____
_____
_____
_____
_____
_____
_____
_____
_____

TODAY I NEED:

_____
_____
_____
_____

TODAY I ASPIRE TO:

_____
_____
_____
_____
_____

Evening Reflections

TODAY I LEARNED:

_____
_____

TODAY I WAS CHALLENGED BY:

_____
_____

TODAY I WAS HAPPY THAT:

_____
_____

DATE _____

Daily Prayers

I'M GRATEFUL FOR:

_____
_____
_____
_____
_____
_____
_____
_____
_____
_____
_____

TODAY I NEED:

_____
_____
_____
_____

TODAY I ASPIRE TO:

_____
_____
_____
_____
_____

Evening Reflections

TODAY I LEARNED:

_____
_____

TODAY I WAS CHALLENGED BY:

_____
_____

TODAY I WAS HAPPY THAT:

_____

DATE _____

Daily Prayers

I'M GRATEFUL FOR:

_____
_____
_____
_____
_____
_____
_____
_____
_____
_____
_____

TODAY I NEED:

_____
_____
_____
_____
_____

TODAY I ASPIRE TO:

_____
_____
_____
_____
_____

Evening Reflections

TODAY I LEARNED:

_____

TODAY I WAS CHALLENGED BY:

_____

TODAY I WAS HAPPY THAT:

_____

Quote of the Day

"GOD CAN HANDLE YOUR DOUBT, ANGER, FEAR, GRIEF, CONFUSION, AND QUESTIONS.
YOU CAN BRING EVERYTHING TO HIM IN PRAYER." — RICK WARREN

DATE _____

Daily Prayers

I'M GRATEFUL FOR:

_____
_____
_____
_____
_____
_____
_____
_____
_____
_____

TODAY I NEED:

_____
_____
_____
_____

TODAY I ASPIRE TO:

_____
_____
_____
_____

Evening Reflections

TODAY I LEARNED:

_____
_____

TODAY I WAS CHALLENGED BY:

_____
_____

TODAY I WAS HAPPY THAT:

_____

DATE _____

Daily Prayers

I'M GRATEFUL FOR:

_____
_____
_____
_____
_____
_____
_____
_____
_____
_____
_____

TODAY I NEED:

_____
_____
_____
_____
_____

TODAY I ASPIRE TO:

_____
_____
_____
_____
_____

Evening Reflections

TODAY I LEARNED:

_____
_____

TODAY I WAS CHALLENGED BY:

_____
_____

TODAY I WAS HAPPY THAT:

_____

DATE _____

Daily Prayers

I'M GRATEFUL FOR:

_____
_____
_____
_____
_____
_____
_____
_____
_____
_____

TODAY I NEED:

_____
_____
_____
_____

TODAY I ASPIRE TO:

_____
_____
_____
_____
_____

Evening Reflections

TODAY I LEARNED:

_____
_____

TODAY I WAS CHALLENGED BY:

_____
_____
_____

TODAY I WAS HAPPY THAT:

_____
_____

DATE_____

Daily Prayers

I'M GRATEFUL FOR:

_____
_____
_____
_____
_____
_____
_____
_____
_____
_____
_____

TODAY I NEED:

_____
_____
_____
_____

TODAY I ASPIRE TO:

_____
_____
_____
_____
_____

Evening Reflections

TODAY I LEARNED:

_____
_____

TODAY I WAS CHALLENGED BY:

_____
_____

TODAY I WAS HAPPY THAT:

_____
_____

DAYS 41 TO 50:

Prayer Is How
We Ask for What We Need

Do not be anxious about anything, but in every situation, by prayer and petition, with thanksgiving, present your requests to God. – Philippians 4:6

One of the worst situations I found myself in was when I could not financially support my children. I was months behind in rent. I was feeding my children cereal with water. I was alone. I was ashamed. I was defeated. I was depressed. I could not sleep. I often cried when I was alone. I hid it from everyone.

Christmas was around the corner. I didn't know what I was going to do. I had separated from my husband, and my kids were already dealing with a whole bunch of changes.

I started to pray for God to show me how to deal with this awful mess I was in. I could not imagine how God would help me.

We didn't have a Christmas tree to put up, so I took a roll of paper someone had given us, unrolled a bunch on the floor, and explained to the kids that we were going to make our tree. They had so much fun drawing out the tree and then decorating it. They were so proud of their creation. We taped the tree, the paper star, and paper baubles on the wall.

Now, the question became, "What gifts would I put under that tree for the children?"

A week before Christmas, one Sunday morning at church, one of the members came up to me, quietly pulled me aside, and handed me an envelope. They told me to open it only after getting home, and they walked away.

In the envelope was $200 and a note that simply read. "Give your children a Christmas. Buy them what they need."

Several days later, the front doorbell sounded; I opened the door, there was no one there. But on the stoop were two bags of groceries. Who had left the bags? To this day, I don't know who they were.

I know that my children and I no longer take anything that God blesses us with for granted. These were all teaching moments for my children and me.

Sometimes, we are called to do things that feel overwhelming. Ask God for direction and wait to see how He moves.

God, thank you for your faithfulness and for answering my prayers! Right now, I'm dealing with (situation or event), and I am feeling overwhelmed. Lord, show me what to do and give me the wisdom to deal with my situation. In Jesus' name, Amen.

Savior, hear my humble cry

Pass Me Not, O Gentle Savior
by Fanny Crosby

Pass me not, O gentle Savior,
Hear my humble cry;
While on others Thou art calling,
Do not pass me by.

Chorus
Saviour, Saviour,
Hear my humble cry.
While on others Thou art calling,
Do not pass me by.

Let me at Thy throne of mercy,
Find a sweet relief.
Kneeling there in deep contrition,
Help my unbelief. (chorus)

Trusting only in Thy merit,
Would I seek Thy face,
Heal my wounded, broken spirit,
Save me by Thy grace. (chorus)

DATE _____

Daily Prayers

I'M GRATEFUL FOR:

_____
_____
_____
_____
_____
_____
_____
_____
_____
_____

TODAY I NEED:

_____
_____
_____

TODAY I ASPIRE TO:

_____
_____
_____
_____

Evening Reflections

TODAY I LEARNED:

_____

TODAY I WAS CHALLENGED BY:

_____

TODAY I WAS HAPPY THAT:

_____

Prayer Tip – Use A Prayer Journal

A JOURNAL WILL HELP YOU FOCUS DURING YOUR PRAYER TIME AND NOTE WHAT AND WHO YOU
HAVE PRAYED FOR AND WHEN. IT WILL HELP YOU LOOK BACK, GIVE THANKS FOR ANSWERED PRAYERS,
AND BE A REMINDER TO CONTINUE PRAYING FOR OTHERS.

DATE_____

Daily Prayers

I'M GRATEFUL FOR:

_____
_____
_____
_____
_____
_____
_____
_____
_____
_____
_____
_____

TODAY I NEED:

_____
_____
_____
_____

TODAY I ASPIRE TO:

_____
_____
_____
_____
_____

Evening Reflections

TODAY I LEARNED:

_____
_____

TODAY I WAS CHALLENGED BY:

_____
_____

TODAY I WAS HAPPY THAT:

_____

DATE _____

Daily Prayers

I'M GRATEFUL FOR:

_____
_____
_____
_____
_____
_____
_____
_____
_____
_____

TODAY I NEED:

_____
_____
_____
_____

TODAY I ASPIRE TO:

_____
_____
_____
_____

Evening Reflections

TODAY I LEARNED:

_____
_____

TODAY I WAS CHALLENGED BY:

_____
_____

TODAY I WAS HAPPY THAT:

_____
_____

DATE_____

Daily Prayers

I'M GRATEFUL FOR:

_____
_____
_____
_____
_____
_____
_____
_____
_____
_____

TODAY I NEED:

_____
_____
_____

TODAY I ASPIRE TO:

_____
_____
_____
_____

⊙○⊙○⊙○⊙○⊙○

Evening Reflections

TODAY I LEARNED:

_____
_____

TODAY I WAS CHALLENGED BY:

_____
_____

TODAY I WAS HAPPY THAT:

_____

DATE _____

Daily Prayers

I'M GRATEFUL FOR:

_____
_____
_____
_____
_____
_____
_____
_____
_____
_____

TODAY I NEED:

_____
_____
_____
_____

TODAY I ASPIRE TO:

_____
_____
_____
_____

Evening Reflections

TODAY I LEARNED:

_____
_____

TODAY I WAS CHALLENGED BY:

_____
_____

TODAY I WAS HAPPY THAT:

_____

DATE_____

Daily Prayers

I'M GRATEFUL FOR:

_____
_____
_____
_____
_____
_____
_____
_____
_____
_____

TODAY I NEED:

_____
_____
_____
_____
_____

TODAY I ASPIRE TO:

_____
_____
_____
_____
_____

Evening Reflections

TODAY I LEARNED:

_____

TODAY I WAS CHALLENGED BY:

_____

TODAY I WAS HAPPY THAT:

_____

Quote of the Day

"TO GET NATIONS BACK ON THEIR FEET,
WE MUST FIRST GET DOWN ON OUR KNEES." — BILLY GRAHAM

DATE_____

Daily Prayers

I'M GRATEFUL FOR:

_____
_____
_____
_____
_____
_____
_____
_____
_____
_____

TODAY I NEED:

_____
_____
_____
_____

TODAY I ASPIRE TO:

_____
_____
_____
_____

Evening Reflections

TODAY I LEARNED:

_____
_____

TODAY I WAS CHALLENGED BY:

_____
_____

TODAY I WAS HAPPY THAT:

_____
_____

DATE _____

Daily Prayers

I'M GRATEFUL FOR:

_____
_____
_____
_____
_____
_____
_____
_____
_____
_____
_____

TODAY I NEED:

_____
_____
_____
_____

TODAY I ASPIRE TO:

_____
_____
_____
_____
_____

Evening Reflections

TODAY I LEARNED:

_____
_____

TODAY I WAS CHALLENGED BY:

_____
_____

TODAY I WAS HAPPY THAT:

_____

DATE _____

Daily Prayers

I'M GRATEFUL FOR:

_____
_____
_____
_____
_____
_____
_____
_____
_____

TODAY I NEED:

_____
_____
_____
_____

TODAY I ASPIRE TO:

_____
_____
_____
_____
_____

Evening Reflections

TODAY I LEARNED:

_____
_____

TODAY I WAS CHALLENGED BY:

_____
_____

TODAY I WAS HAPPY THAT:

_____

DATE _____

Daily Prayers

I'M GRATEFUL FOR:

_____
_____
_____
_____
_____
_____
_____
_____
_____
_____

TODAY I NEED:

_____
_____
_____
_____

TODAY I ASPIRE TO:

_____
_____
_____
_____
_____

Evening Reflections

TODAY I LEARNED:

_____
_____

TODAY I WAS CHALLENGED BY:

_____
_____

TODAY I WAS HAPPY THAT:

_____
_____

DAYS 51 TO 60:

Prayer Is How
We Confess Our Sins

If we confess our sins, he is faithful and just to forgive us our sins
and to cleanse us from all unrighteousness. – 1 John 1:9

I opened the door to my home. It was 4:30 a.m., much later than I had planned to be out. I hoped my children would not wake up and find me just getting home.

I vowed to make up for my sin. I planned something special for my Sunday School class. I would fix this, get things back in order. I had to!

Thoughts of my family and church friends made me shudder. What would they think of me if they discovered my secret? Everyone thought I had my life so together. How could I face them if they knew! I felt so ashamed. I felt powerless to stop what I knew in my heart was wrong. I am a hypocrite. This is the last time. I know I can stop. I know I can; I have to!

This night was not the first time I had made this vow. It was a vow I had been making more and more frequently, only to break it soon after.

Sexual addiction is a secret that has been around since biblical times. The religious community is quick to point a finger and condemn this sin, as it should be, but it has been unwilling or unable to understand the sexual sinner and offer them the help they so desperately need.

"Knowing you are a sex addict doesn't mean you are bad or perverted or hopeless. It means that you may have a disease, an obsession from which you may be healed." – Dr. Patrick Carne

The confession of sin comes with the desire to stop the sin. God's forgiveness does not mean there won't be consequences. If we have fellowship with the Father and with His Son, the Lord Jesus Christ, we will walk in the light and not sin through the Word of God. The sad reality is, those of us who are saved do not always walk cautiously. God knows our shortcomings and has provided a way for us to confess and ask for forgiveness of our sins.

Confession is the acknowledgment of our sin and, with it, the desire to stop the sin. No child of God would be content to commit and live with sin. It grieves the heart of God, and it also grieves the heart of the saved person. But God is good, and He promises to cleanse the unrighteousness in our lives.

God, help me to stop hiding my sin.
Forgive me for my sins and set me free!
In Jesus' name, Amen.

Breathe on Me, Breath of God
by Edwin Hatch

Breathe on me, Breath of God,
Fill me with life anew,
That I may love what Thou dost love,
And do what Thou wouldst do.

Breathe on me, Breath of God,
Until my heart is pure,
Until my will is one with Thine,
To do and to endure.

Breathe on me, breath of God,
Blend all my soul with Thine,
Until this earthly part of me
Glows with Thy fire divine.

Breathe on me, breath of God,
So shall I never die,
But live with Thee the perfect life
Of Thine eternity.

DATE _____

Daily Prayers

I'M GRATEFUL FOR:

_____
_____
_____
_____
_____
_____
_____
_____
_____
_____
_____

TODAY I NEED:

_____
_____
_____
_____

TODAY I ASPIRE TO:

_____
_____
_____
_____
_____

Evening Reflections

TODAY I LEARNED:

_____

TODAY I WAS CHALLENGED BY:

_____

TODAY I WAS HAPPY THAT:

_____

Prayer Tip – Be Intentional

USING A PRAYER LIST AND JOURNAL WILL GIVE SUBSTANCE TO YOUR
PRAYERS AND HELP YOU AVOID OVERGENERALIZED PRAYERS.

DATE _____

Daily Prayers

I'M GRATEFUL FOR:

_____
_____
_____
_____
_____
_____
_____
_____
_____
_____
_____
_____

TODAY I NEED:

_____
_____
_____
_____

TODAY I ASPIRE TO:

_____
_____
_____
_____
_____

Evening Reflections

TODAY I LEARNED:

_____
_____

TODAY I WAS CHALLENGED BY:

_____
_____

TODAY I WAS HAPPY THAT:

_____
_____

Daily Prayers

I'M GRATEFUL FOR:

_____
_____
_____
_____
_____
_____
_____
_____
_____
_____
_____

TODAY I NEED:

_____
_____
_____
_____

TODAY I ASPIRE TO:

_____
_____
_____
_____
_____

Evening Reflections

TODAY I LEARNED:

_____
_____

TODAY I WAS CHALLENGED BY:

_____
_____

TODAY I WAS HAPPY THAT:

_____
_____

DATE_____

Daily Prayers

I'M GRATEFUL FOR:

_____
_____
_____
_____
_____
_____
_____
_____
_____
_____

TODAY I NEED:

_____
_____
_____
_____

TODAY I ASPIRE TO:

_____
_____
_____
_____
_____

Evening Reflections

TODAY I LEARNED:

_____
_____

TODAY I WAS CHALLENGED BY:

_____
_____

TODAY I WAS HAPPY THAT:

_____

DATE _____

Daily Prayers

I'M GRATEFUL FOR:

_____

_____

_____

_____

_____

_____

_____

_____

_____

_____

TODAY I NEED:

_____

_____

_____

TODAY I ASPIRE TO:

_____

_____

_____

_____

Evening Reflections

TODAY I LEARNED:

_____

_____

TODAY I WAS CHALLENGED BY:

_____

_____

TODAY I WAS HAPPY THAT:

_____

_____

DATE_____

Daily Prayers

I'M GRATEFUL FOR:

_____
_____
_____
_____
_____
_____
_____
_____
_____
_____
_____

TODAY I NEED:

_____
_____
_____

TODAY I ASPIRE TO:

_____
_____
_____
_____

०◉०◉०◉०◉०◉०

Evening Reflections

TODAY I LEARNED:

_____

TODAY I WAS CHALLENGED BY:

_____

TODAY I WAS HAPPY THAT:

_____

Quote of the Day
"A DAY WITHOUT PRAYER IS A DAY WITHOUT BLESSING, AND A
LIFE WITHOUT PRAYER IS A LIFE WITHOUT POWER." — EDWIN HARVEY

DATE _____

Daily Prayers

I'M GRATEFUL FOR:

_____
_____
_____
_____
_____
_____
_____
_____
_____
_____
_____

TODAY I NEED:

_____
_____
_____
_____

TODAY I ASPIRE TO:

_____
_____
_____
_____

Evening Reflections

TODAY I LEARNED:

_____
_____

TODAY I WAS CHALLENGED BY:

_____
_____

TODAY I WAS HAPPY THAT:

_____

DATE _____

Daily Prayers

I'M GRATEFUL FOR:

_____
_____
_____
_____
_____
_____
_____
_____
_____
_____
_____

TODAY I NEED:

_____
_____
_____
_____

TODAY I ASPIRE TO:

_____
_____
_____
_____
_____

Evening Reflections

TODAY I LEARNED:

_____
_____

TODAY I WAS CHALLENGED BY:

_____
_____

TODAY I WAS HAPPY THAT:

_____
_____

DATE _____

Daily Prayers

I'M GRATEFUL FOR:

_____
_____
_____
_____
_____
_____
_____
_____
_____
_____

TODAY I NEED:

_____
_____
_____
_____

TODAY I ASPIRE TO:

_____
_____
_____
_____

○◉○◉○◉○◉○◉○◉○

Evening Reflections

TODAY I LEARNED:

_____
_____

TODAY I WAS CHALLENGED BY:

_____
_____

TODAY I WAS HAPPY THAT:

_____
_____

DATE _____

Daily Prayers

I'M GRATEFUL FOR:

_____
_____
_____
_____
_____
_____
_____
_____
_____
_____

TODAY I NEED:

_____
_____
_____
_____

TODAY I ASPIRE TO:

_____
_____
_____
_____

Evening Reflections

TODAY I LEARNED:

_____
_____

TODAY I WAS CHALLENGED BY:

_____

TODAY I WAS HAPPY THAT:

_____

DAYS 61 TO 70:

Prayer Is How
We Receive Salvation

And it shall come to pass that everyone who calls upon the name of the Lord shall be saved. — Acts 2:21

In my darkest days, when the noise of sin was so loud in my life, I could not hear the Lord calling me to find rest in Him. I had surrounded myself with so much worldly noise—it was the only way to silence that tiny voice in my head. Yet, my instinct was to cry out to the Lord, looking for a way out of the dark hole I'd fallen in.

After a night of clubbing, I crawled into bed in the wee hours of the morning, so drunk that I blacked out and couldn't remember how I got home or who I'd been with. I was on the path of self-destruction. Self-loathing. I was alone and scared.

If I continued this deadly double life, I would not be able to cheat death for much longer. I was playing Russian roulette with my life, and it wasn't only my own, but the lives of three precious children that I was responsible for.

I nor anyone else could save me. That night, as my body writhed in pain and my mind was in turmoil, "In my distress I called upon the Lord; to my God I cried for help. From his temple he heard my voice, and my cry to him reached his ears" (Psalm 18:6).

The all-merciful and forgiving Lord heard my pleas that night, "he rescued me, because he delighted in me" (Psalm 18:19b).

Why do we need to call upon the Lord? Because we are stuck in the dark hole of sin that we cannot crawl out of ourselves, no matter how hard and long we try. We are trapped in the prison of sin, and we do not have a "get out of jail" card. We are enslaved to the cruel taskmaster of sin's addiction, and we need our Redeemer to set us free.

Jesus saved my life from self-destructive ways, cured me of alcoholism. I owe my life to Him. Not one of us is past redemption. Not one of us has done something so bad that our Lord and Savior will not forgive us. Not one of us who calls His name and seeks Him is turned away. Every one of us who calls on the Lord's name will be saved.

Lord, thank you for dying on the cross for my sins. I confess my sins and ask for your forgiveness. Please come into my heart today as my Lord and Savior. Help me live for You and help me walk daily in Your footsteps from this day forward. Thank you, Lord, for saving me and for answering my prayer. In Jesus' name. Amen.

Search me, O God
by James E. Orr

Search me, O God, and know my heart today;
Try me, O Savior, know my thoughts, I pray.
See if there be some wicked way in me;
Cleanse me from every sin and set me free.

I praise thee, Lord, for cleansing me from sin;
Fulfill thy Word, and make me pure within.
Fill me with fire where once I burned with shame;
Grant my desire to magnify thy name.

3 Lord, take my life and make it wholly thine;
Fill my poor heart with thy great love divine.
Take all my will, my passion, self, and pride;
I now surrender; Lord, in me abide.

DATE _____

Daily Prayers

I'M GRATEFUL FOR:

_____
_____
_____
_____
_____
_____
_____
_____
_____
_____
_____

TODAY I NEED:

_____
_____
_____
_____

TODAY I ASPIRE TO:

_____
_____
_____
_____
_____

Evening Reflections

TODAY I LEARNED:

_____

TODAY I WAS CHALLENGED BY:

_____

TODAY I WAS HAPPY THAT:

_____

Prayer Tip – Pray Out Loud

I FIND PRAYING OUT LOUD HELPS ME FOCUS. SOMETIMES WHEN I AM ANXIOUS, STRESSED,
OR TIRED AND I PRAY SILENTLY I WILL LET MY MIND WANDER AND FALL ASLEEP MID-SENTENCE.

Daily Prayers

I'M GRATEFUL FOR:

_____
_____
_____
_____
_____
_____
_____
_____
_____
_____
_____

DATE _____

TODAY I NEED:

_____
_____
_____

TODAY I ASPIRE TO:

_____
_____
_____
_____
_____

Evening Reflections

TODAY I LEARNED:

_____
_____

TODAY I WAS CHALLENGED BY:

_____
_____

TODAY I WAS HAPPY THAT:

_____

DATE _____

Daily Prayers

I'M GRATEFUL FOR:

_____
_____
_____
_____
_____
_____
_____
_____
_____
_____
_____

TODAY I NEED:

_____
_____
_____
_____
_____

TODAY I ASPIRE TO:

_____
_____
_____
_____
_____

Evening Reflections

TODAY I LEARNED:

_____
_____

TODAY I WAS CHALLENGED BY:

_____
_____

TODAY I WAS HAPPY THAT:

_____

DATE _____

Daily Prayers

I'M GRATEFUL FOR:

_____
_____
_____
_____
_____
_____
_____
_____
_____
_____
_____

TODAY I NEED:

_____
_____
_____
_____

TODAY I ASPIRE TO:

_____
_____
_____
_____

Evening Reflections

TODAY I LEARNED:

_____
_____

TODAY I WAS CHALLENGED BY:

_____
_____

TODAY I WAS HAPPY THAT:

_____

DATE_____

Daily Prayers

I'M GRATEFUL FOR:

_____
_____
_____
_____
_____
_____
_____
_____
_____
_____
_____

TODAY I NEED:

_____
_____
_____

TODAY I ASPIRE TO:

_____
_____
_____
_____

◦❀◦❀◦❀◦❀◦❀◦

Evening Reflections

TODAY I LEARNED:

_____
_____

TODAY I WAS CHALLENGED BY:

_____
_____

TODAY I WAS HAPPY THAT:

_____
_____

DATE _____

Daily Prayers

I'M GRATEFUL FOR:

_____
_____
_____
_____
_____
_____
_____
_____
_____
_____

TODAY I NEED:

_____
_____
_____
_____

TODAY I ASPIRE TO:

_____
_____
_____
_____

◦ⓞ◦ⓞ◦ⓞ◦ⓞ◦ⓞ◦

Evening Reflections

TODAY I LEARNED:

_____

TODAY I WAS CHALLENGED BY:

_____

TODAY I WAS HAPPY THAT:

_____

Quote of the Day
"EVERY GREAT MOVEMENT OF GOD CAN BE TRACED
TO A KNEELING FIGURE." — D. L. MOODY

DATE _____

Daily Prayers

I'M GRATEFUL FOR:

_____
_____
_____
_____
_____
_____
_____
_____
_____
_____
_____

TODAY I NEED:

_____
_____
_____
_____

TODAY I ASPIRE TO:

_____
_____
_____
_____
_____

Evening Reflections

TODAY I LEARNED:

_____
_____

TODAY I WAS CHALLENGED BY:

_____
_____

TODAY I WAS HAPPY THAT:

_____
_____

DATE_____

Daily Prayers

I'M GRATEFUL FOR:

_____
_____
_____
_____
_____
_____
_____
_____
_____
_____
_____

TODAY I NEED:

_____
_____
_____
_____

TODAY I ASPIRE TO:

_____
_____
_____
_____
_____

Evening Reflections

TODAY I LEARNED:

_____
_____

TODAY I WAS CHALLENGED BY:

_____

TODAY I WAS HAPPY THAT:

_____

DATE_____

Daily Prayers

I'M GRATEFUL FOR:

_____
_____
_____
_____
_____
_____
_____
_____
_____
_____

TODAY I NEED:

_____
_____
_____
_____

TODAY I ASPIRE TO:

_____
_____
_____
_____

Evening Reflections

TODAY I LEARNED:

_____
_____

TODAY I WAS CHALLENGED BY:

_____
_____

TODAY I WAS HAPPY THAT:

_____
_____

Daily Prayers

I'M GRATEFUL FOR:

_____
_____
_____
_____
_____
_____
_____
_____
_____
_____

TODAY I NEED:

_____
_____
_____
_____

TODAY I ASPIRE TO:

_____
_____
_____
_____

Evening Reflections

TODAY I LEARNED:

_____
_____

TODAY I WAS CHALLENGED BY:

_____
_____

TODAY I WAS HAPPY THAT:

_____

DAYS 71 TO 80:

Prayer Is How
We Intercede for Others

First of all, then, I urge that requests, prayers, intercessions, and thanks be offered on behalf of all people. – 1 Timothy 2:1

I grew up in a family of prayer warriors. My paternal grandparents set that example for me at an early age. Saturday sleepovers meant that we would sit around in the living room reading the Bible and spend time in prayer in the evening. Those prayers were filled with names that I did not recognize.

As I became an adult, those prayers included my name. When I went through a difficult breakup and divorce, my family's name was lifted in prayer and petition. After my divorce, life took a turn for the worst and was filled with darkness, and my prayers stopped. Unbeknownst to me, my grandmother, my parents, and other family members were on their knees praying for the prodigal daughter.

The party life I craved and was addicted to did not dull the pain and stop the voices in my head; instead, the sadness and pain increased. Alcohol dulled the noise for a while. Sex was a bandage on a festering wound that only made things worse.

Looking back, I wonder how I could have been so careless to put the lives of my children in jeopardy. I could have died as a direct result of my choices. When you are walking in the path of sin and darkness, you cannot see what is happening around you.

With every fiber of my being, I believe that the prayers that my family uttered on my behalf saved me from many dangerous situations. When I look back, I wonder how I walked away from them. I took chances that make the hair on the back of my neck stand up today.

Not only did God forgive my sins and heal my aching soul, but He gave me a chance to use my story to reach out and help others. I now spend time on my knees interceding on others' behalf.

God, I know (name) has sinned against you. I know that You are a merciful and compassionate God. Restore them to fellowship with You so they can walk your righteous ways. In Jesus' name, Amen.

Melt me,
mold me,
Fill me,
use me.

Spirit of the Living God
by Daniel Iverson

Spirit of the Living God,
Fall fresh on me.
Spirit of the Living God,
Fall fresh on me.
Melt me, mold me,
Fill me, use me.
Spirit of the Living God,
Fall fresh on me.

DATE _____

Daily Prayers

I'M GRATEFUL FOR:

_____
_____
_____
_____
_____
_____
_____
_____
_____
_____

TODAY I NEED:

_____
_____
_____

TODAY I ASPIRE TO:

_____
_____
_____
_____

Evening Reflections

TODAY I LEARNED:

_____

TODAY I WAS CHALLENGED BY:

_____

TODAY I WAS HAPPY THAT:

_____

Prayer Tip - Find A Prayer Partner

JOIN IN PRAYER WITH SOMEONE WHO WILL SHARE THE BURDEN OF PRAYER WITH YOU. PRAYING WITH SOMEONE WILL KEEP YOU ACCOUNTABLE AND ALSO WILL BE AN ENCOURAGEMENT. JESUS TELLS HIS DISCIPLES THAT THEY SHOULD GET TOGETHER AND ASK TOGETHER (MATTHEW 18:19-20).

DATE _____

Daily Prayers

I'M GRATEFUL FOR:

_____
_____
_____
_____
_____
_____
_____
_____
_____
_____

TODAY I NEED:

_____
_____
_____
_____

TODAY I ASPIRE TO:

_____
_____
_____
_____
_____

Evening Reflections

TODAY I LEARNED:

_____
_____

TODAY I WAS CHALLENGED BY:

_____
_____

TODAY I WAS HAPPY THAT:

_____

Daily Prayers

DATE _____

I'M GRATEFUL FOR:

_____
_____
_____
_____
_____
_____
_____
_____
_____

TODAY I NEED:

_____
_____
_____

TODAY I ASPIRE TO:

_____
_____
_____
_____

Evening Reflections

TODAY I LEARNED:

_____
_____

TODAY I WAS CHALLENGED BY:

_____
_____

TODAY I WAS HAPPY THAT:

_____
_____

DATE _____

Daily Prayers

I'M GRATEFUL FOR:

_____
_____
_____
_____
_____
_____
_____
_____
_____
_____

TODAY I NEED:

_____
_____
_____
_____

TODAY I ASPIRE TO:

_____
_____
_____
_____
_____

Evening Reflections

TODAY I LEARNED:

_____
_____

TODAY I WAS CHALLENGED BY:

_____
_____

TODAY I WAS HAPPY THAT:

_____

DATE _____

Daily Prayers

I'M GRATEFUL FOR:

_____
_____
_____
_____
_____
_____
_____
_____
_____
_____

TODAY I NEED:

_____
_____
_____
_____

TODAY I ASPIRE TO:

_____
_____
_____
_____
_____

◦◉◦◉◦◉◦◉◦◉◦

Evening Reflections

TODAY I LEARNED:

_____
_____

TODAY I WAS CHALLENGED BY:

_____
_____

TODAY I WAS HAPPY THAT:

_____
_____

DATE _____

Daily Prayers

I'M GRATEFUL FOR:

_____
_____
_____
_____
_____
_____
_____
_____
_____
_____
_____

TODAY I NEED:

_____
_____
_____
_____

TODAY I ASPIRE TO:

_____
_____
_____
_____

Evening Reflections

TODAY I LEARNED:

_____

TODAY I WAS CHALLENGED BY:

_____

TODAY I WAS HAPPY THAT:

_____

Quote of the Day

"IS PRAYER YOUR STEERING WHEEL OR YOUR SPARE TIRE?"
— CORRIE TEN BOOM

DATE _____

Daily Prayers

I'M GRATEFUL FOR:

_____
_____
_____
_____
_____
_____
_____
_____
_____

TODAY I NEED:

_____
_____
_____

TODAY I ASPIRE TO:

_____
_____
_____
_____

Evening Reflections

TODAY I LEARNED:

_____
_____

TODAY I WAS CHALLENGED BY:

_____
_____

TODAY I WAS HAPPY THAT:

_____

Daily Prayers

I'M GRATEFUL FOR:

_____
_____
_____
_____
_____
_____
_____
_____
_____
_____
_____

TODAY I NEED:

_____
_____
_____
_____

TODAY I ASPIRE TO:

_____
_____
_____
_____

Evening Reflections

TODAY I LEARNED:

_____
_____

TODAY I WAS CHALLENGED BY:

_____
_____

TODAY I WAS HAPPY THAT:

_____
_____

DATE_____

Daily Prayers

I'M GRATEFUL FOR:

_____
_____
_____
_____
_____
_____
_____
_____
_____
_____
_____

TODAY I NEED:

_____
_____
_____
_____

TODAY I ASPIRE TO:

_____
_____
_____
_____
_____

Evening Reflections

TODAY I LEARNED:

_____
_____

TODAY I WAS CHALLENGED BY:

_____
_____

TODAY I WAS HAPPY THAT:

_____
_____

DATE _____

Daily Prayers

I'M GRATEFUL FOR:

_____
_____
_____
_____
_____
_____
_____
_____
_____
_____
_____
_____

TODAY I NEED:

_____
_____
_____
_____

TODAY I ASPIRE TO:

_____
_____
_____
_____
_____

Evening Reflections

TODAY I LEARNED:

_____

TODAY I WAS CHALLENGED BY:

_____
_____

TODAY I WAS HAPPY THAT:

_____

DAYS 81 TO 90:

Prayer Is How
We Resist Temptation

Watch and pray so that you will not fall into temptation.
The spirit is willing, but the flesh is weak. – Matthew 26:41

My divorce left a massive void in my life. I felt I hadn't been good enough. I hadn't been enough. If I had been prettier, more intelligent, sexier, and so on, my husband would not have divorced me. I saw this gaping hole in my life that I needed to fill. I tried to do this through sexual relationships. However, those encounters made the hole bigger and deeper instead of filling the emptiness. Sexual sin is an addiction that only God can get rid of.

We all have been tempted at some point in our lives. It could be as simple as buying something we don't need to something that has devastating consequences, such as a sexual affair.

There are two parts to sexual temptation. There's the physical craving, and then there's the emotional need. The physical craving itself is not sinful, and God gave us those desires. But unless we are married, we must resist those desires. Emotional needs are fully satisfied by God. He is more than enough for our emotional longings.

"Whom have I in heaven but you? And there is nothing on earth that I desire besides you" (Psalm 73:25).

Sexual temptation can come to anyone. If you are married and going through difficulties in your relationship, the temptation can be that co-worker who gives you the attention you crave, or perhaps porn has taken root in your life. Remove all sources of temptation from your life.

Avoid feeding your unholy desires. Stay away from situations that encourage this behavior. Get an accountability partner.

If someone you love is battling temptations, pray for them. Pray that if they fail to resist temptation, God will redeem them. Pray for God to fill them with the power to start over.

God, I pray for (name). I know they're enduring a lot of temptation right now, and You see that. I ask, strengthen this person in Your name. Give them the wisdom to walk away from temptation and if they fall prey to it, show them how to repent and turn back to You. In Jesus' name, Amen.

Take my love, my God, I pour at Thy feet its treasure store;

Take My Life and Let It Be
by Frances R. Havergal

Take my life and let it be
Consecrated, Lord to Thee;
Take my hands and let them move
At the impulse of Thy love,
At the impulse of Thy love.

Take my feet, and let them be
Swift and beautiful for Thee;
Take my voice and let me sing
Always, only for my King,
Always, only for my King.

Take my lips and let them be
Filled with praises, Lord to Thee,
Take my silver and my gold,
Not a mite would I withhold,
Not a mite would I withhold.

Take my love, my Lord, I pour
At Thy feet its treasure store;
Take myself and I will be
Ever, only, all for Thee,
Ever, only, all for Thee.

DATE _____

Daily Prayers

I'M GRATEFUL FOR:

_____
_____
_____
_____
_____
_____
_____
_____
_____
_____

TODAY I NEED:

_____
_____
_____
_____

TODAY I ASPIRE TO:

_____
_____
_____
_____
_____

∘⊙∘⊙∘⊙∘⊙∘⊙∘

Evening Reflections

TODAY I LEARNED:

_____

TODAY I WAS CHALLENGED BY:

_____

TODAY I WAS HAPPY THAT:

_____

Prayer Tip – Use Scripture

IF YOU STRUGGLE AND CANNOT FOCUS, USE PRAYERS FROM THE BIBLE.

Daily Prayers

I'M GRATEFUL FOR:

_____
_____
_____
_____
_____
_____
_____
_____
_____
_____

TODAY I NEED:

_____
_____
_____
_____

TODAY I ASPIRE TO:

_____
_____
_____
_____

Evening Reflections

TODAY I LEARNED:

_____
_____

TODAY I WAS CHALLENGED BY:

_____
_____

TODAY I WAS HAPPY THAT:

_____
_____

DATE _____

Daily Prayers

I'M GRATEFUL FOR:

_____
_____
_____
_____
_____
_____
_____
_____
_____
_____

TODAY I NEED:

_____
_____
_____
_____

TODAY I ASPIRE TO:

_____
_____
_____
_____
_____

Evening Reflections

TODAY I LEARNED:

_____
_____

TODAY I WAS CHALLENGED BY:

_____
_____

TODAY I WAS HAPPY THAT:

_____

DATE _____

Daily Prayers

I'M GRATEFUL FOR:

_____
_____
_____
_____
_____
_____
_____
_____
_____
_____
_____
_____

TODAY I NEED:

_____
_____
_____
_____
_____

TODAY I ASPIRE TO:

_____
_____
_____
_____
_____

Evening Reflections

TODAY I LEARNED:

_____
_____

TODAY I WAS CHALLENGED BY:

_____
_____

TODAY I WAS HAPPY THAT:

_____

DATE _____

Daily Prayers

I'M GRATEFUL FOR:

_____
_____
_____
_____
_____
_____
_____
_____
_____
_____

TODAY I NEED:

_____
_____
_____
_____

TODAY I ASPIRE TO:

_____
_____
_____
_____

Evening Reflections

TODAY I LEARNED:

_____
_____

TODAY I WAS CHALLENGED BY:

_____
_____

TODAY I WAS HAPPY THAT:

_____
_____

DATE _____

Daily Prayers

I'M GRATEFUL FOR:

_____
_____
_____
_____
_____
_____
_____
_____
_____
_____
_____

TODAY I NEED:

_____
_____
_____
_____

TODAY I ASPIRE TO:

_____
_____
_____
_____

∘◉∘◉∘◉∘◉∘◉∘

Evening Reflections

TODAY I LEARNED:

_____

TODAY I WAS CHALLENGED BY:

_____

TODAY I WAS HAPPY THAT:

_____

Quote of the Day

IF THE HEART WANDERS OR IS DISTRACTED, BRING IT BACK TO THE POINT QUITE GENTLY AND REPLACE IT
TENDERLY IN ITS MASTER'S PRESENCE. AND EVEN IF YOU DID NOTHING DURING THE WHOLE OF YOUR HOUR BUT
BRING YOUR HEART BACK AND PLACE IT AGAIN IN OUR LORD'S PRESENCE, THOUGH IT WENT AWAY EVERY TIME
YOU BROUGHT IT BACK, YOUR HOUR WILL BE VERY WELL EMPLOYED. — ST. FRANCIS DE SALES

DATE _____

Daily Prayers

I'M GRATEFUL FOR:

_____
_____
_____
_____
_____
_____
_____
_____
_____
_____

TODAY I NEED:

_____
_____
_____
_____

TODAY I ASPIRE TO:

_____
_____
_____
_____
_____

Evening Reflections

TODAY I LEARNED:

_____
_____

TODAY I WAS CHALLENGED BY:

_____
_____

TODAY I WAS HAPPY THAT:

_____
_____

DATE _____

Daily Prayers

I'M GRATEFUL FOR:

_____
_____
_____
_____
_____
_____
_____
_____
_____
_____
_____
_____

TODAY I NEED:

_____
_____
_____
_____
_____

TODAY I ASPIRE TO:

_____
_____
_____
_____
_____

Evening Reflections

TODAY I LEARNED:

_____
_____

TODAY I WAS CHALLENGED BY:

_____
_____

TODAY I WAS HAPPY THAT:

_____
_____

DATE _____

Daily Prayers

I'M GRATEFUL FOR:

_____
_____
_____
_____
_____
_____
_____
_____
_____
_____
_____

TODAY I NEED:

_____
_____
_____
_____

TODAY I ASPIRE TO:

_____
_____
_____
_____

Evening Reflections

TODAY I LEARNED:

_____
_____

TODAY I WAS CHALLENGED BY:

_____
_____

TODAY I WAS HAPPY THAT:

_____

DATE _____

Daily Prayers

I'M GRATEFUL FOR:

_____
_____
_____
_____
_____
_____
_____
_____
_____
_____
_____

TODAY I NEED:

_____
_____
_____
_____

TODAY I ASPIRE TO:

_____
_____
_____
_____
_____

Evening Reflections

TODAY I LEARNED:

_____
_____

TODAY I WAS CHALLENGED BY:

_____
_____

TODAY I WAS HAPPY THAT:

_____
_____

DAYS 91 TO 100:

Prayer Is How
We Bless Our Enemies

But I say to you who hear, Love your enemies, do good to those who hate you, bless those who curse you, pray for those who abuse you. – Luke 6:27–28

While going through the worst of my divorce, family members I loved as though they were my flesh and blood turned on me. They wrote me letters accusing me of all sorts of things. I also received letters and phone calls from church members calling me all kinds of names, blaming me for my marriage situation.

I didn't know who to turn to. This was a dirty secret I kept close to my heart for years. I was ashamed of how they had treated me. I believed it was a reflection of who I was.

As I grew closer to the Lord, I asked him, "How can Jesus tell me to love my enemies? Doesn't he know all that I have done for these people, and they are repaying me by turning on me?"

Remember Joseph? His enemies were his flesh and blood, his brothers. What did he ever do to them? Their malice came from jealousy. Years later, in Genesis 50:20, Joseph says, "As for you, you meant evil against me, but God meant it for good, to bring it about that many people should be kept alive, as they are today."

God allowed the events in Joseph's life to take place because he had bigger and better plans for Joseph. The same things apply in our lives. God has a much grander plan than what we can picture for ourselves.

It took me years of reflection and prayer to be able to pray for them finally and to forgive them truly. Today, I am grateful to God for relationships that have mended only because of His graciousness.

Do not mistreat those who mistreat you. Pray for those who mistreat you, speak graciously of them, and do good for them. Pray so that God will change their lives and they will repent. Stephen is a tremendous and powerful example of this in Acts 7, as the people stoned him to death, he prayed for them.

God, I have been hurt by what (name) is doing to me. I want to get even and hurt in return. But by the power of Your Spirit, help me to forgive. I lay down my life just as Stephen did. Please help me forgive (name) for hurting me. Show them great mercy and kindness. In Jesus' name, Amen.

Thou art
the Potter,
I am
the clay

Have Thine Own Way, Lord
by Adelaide Pollard

Have Thine own way Lord
Have Thine own way
Thou art the potter I am the clay
Mold me and make me after Thy will
While I am waiting yielded and still

Have Thine own way Lord
Have Thine own way
Search me and try me Master today
Whiter than snow Lord wash me just now
As in Thy presence humbly I bow

Have Thine own way Lord
Have Thine own way
Hold over my being absolute sway
Filled with Thy spirit till all can see
Christ only always living in me

DATE _____

Daily Prayers

I'M GRATEFUL FOR:

_____
_____
_____
_____
_____
_____
_____
_____
_____
_____

TODAY I NEED:

_____
_____
_____
_____

TODAY I ASPIRE TO:

_____
_____
_____
_____
_____

◦ ❀ ◦ ❀ ◦ ❀ ◦ ❀ ◦ ❀ ◦

Evening Reflections

TODAY I LEARNED:

_____

TODAY I WAS CHALLENGED BY:

_____

TODAY I WAS HAPPY THAT:

_____

Prayer Tip – Change It Up

THERE WILL BE SEASONS IN YOUR LIFE WHERE REGULAR PRAYER TIME WILL NOT BE POSSIBLE. SING SONGS,
OR IF YOU CAN'T STAND YOUR VOICE, LISTEN TO UPLIFTING SONGS OF PRAISE. MEMORIZE SCRIPTURE; THESE
WILL COME IN HANDY WHEN DEALING WITH LIFE.

DATE _____

Daily Prayers

I'M GRATEFUL FOR:

_____
_____
_____
_____
_____
_____
_____
_____
_____
_____
_____
_____

TODAY I NEED:

_____
_____
_____
_____

TODAY I ASPIRE TO:

_____
_____
_____
_____
_____

Evening Reflections

TODAY I LEARNED:

_____
_____

TODAY I WAS CHALLENGED BY:

_____
_____

TODAY I WAS HAPPY THAT:

_____
_____

Daily Prayers

DATE_____

I'M GRATEFUL FOR:

_____
_____
_____
_____
_____
_____
_____
_____
_____
_____

TODAY I NEED:

_____
_____
_____
_____

TODAY I ASPIRE TO:

_____
_____
_____
_____

Evening Reflections

TODAY I LEARNED:

_____
_____

TODAY I WAS CHALLENGED BY:

_____
_____

TODAY I WAS HAPPY THAT:

_____
_____

Daily Prayers

I'M GRATEFUL FOR:

_____
_____
_____
_____
_____
_____
_____
_____
_____
_____
_____

TODAY I NEED:

_____
_____
_____
_____

TODAY I ASPIRE TO:

_____
_____
_____
_____

Evening Reflections

TODAY I LEARNED:

_____
_____

TODAY I WAS CHALLENGED BY:

_____
_____

TODAY I WAS HAPPY THAT:

_____
_____

DATE _____

Daily Prayers

I'M GRATEFUL FOR:

_____
_____
_____
_____
_____
_____
_____
_____
_____

TODAY I NEED:

_____
_____
_____
_____

TODAY I ASPIRE TO:

_____
_____
_____
_____

Evening Reflections

TODAY I LEARNED:

_____
_____

TODAY I WAS CHALLENGED BY:

_____
_____

TODAY I WAS HAPPY THAT:

_____
_____

DATE _____

Daily Prayers

I'M GRATEFUL FOR:

_____
_____
_____
_____
_____
_____
_____
_____
_____
_____
_____
_____

TODAY I NEED:

_____
_____
_____
_____

TODAY I ASPIRE TO:

_____
_____
_____
_____
_____

Evening Reflections

TODAY I LEARNED:

_____

TODAY I WAS CHALLENGED BY:

_____

TODAY I WAS HAPPY THAT:

_____

Quote of the Day

"WHAT WINGS ARE TO A BIRD AND SAILS TO A SHIP,
SO IS PRAYER TO THE SOUL." — CORRIE TEN BOOM

DATE _____

Daily Prayers

I'M GRATEFUL FOR:

_____
_____
_____
_____
_____
_____
_____
_____
_____
_____

TODAY I NEED:

_____
_____
_____
_____

TODAY I ASPIRE TO:

_____
_____
_____
_____

Evening Reflections

TODAY I LEARNED:

_____
_____

TODAY I WAS CHALLENGED BY:

_____
_____

TODAY I WAS HAPPY THAT:

_____
_____

DATE _____

Daily Prayers

I'M GRATEFUL FOR:

_____
_____
_____
_____
_____
_____
_____
_____
_____
_____
_____
_____
_____

TODAY I NEED:

_____
_____
_____
_____
_____

TODAY I ASPIRE TO:

_____
_____
_____
_____
_____

Evening Reflections

TODAY I LEARNED:

_____
_____

TODAY I WAS CHALLENGED BY:

_____
_____

TODAY I WAS HAPPY THAT:

_____
_____

DATE _____

Daily Prayers

I'M GRATEFUL FOR:

_____
_____
_____
_____
_____
_____
_____
_____
_____
_____

TODAY I NEED:

_____
_____
_____
_____

TODAY I ASPIRE TO:

_____
_____
_____
_____
_____

Evening Reflections

TODAY I LEARNED:

_____
_____

TODAY I WAS CHALLENGED BY:

_____
_____

TODAY I WAS HAPPY THAT:

_____
_____

DATE _____

Daily Prayers

I'M GRATEFUL FOR:

_____
_____
_____
_____
_____
_____
_____
_____
_____
_____
_____

TODAY I NEED:

_____
_____
_____

TODAY I ASPIRE TO:

_____
_____
_____
_____

Evening Reflections

TODAY I LEARNED:

_____
_____

TODAY I WAS CHALLENGED BY:

_____
_____

TODAY I WAS HAPPY THAT:

_____

Prayer Log

Prayer Log

NAME	DATE	AREA OF NEED

Is any one of you in trouble? He should pray. Is anyone happy? Let him sing songs of praise. – James 5:13

TIMELINE	FOLLOW UP	OUTCOME

Prayer Log

NAME	DATE	AREA OF NEED

And pray in the Spirit on all occasions with all kinds of prayers and requests. With this in mind, be alert and always keep on praying for all the Lord's people. — Matthew 6:10

TIMELINE	FOLLOW UP	OUTCOME

Prayer Log

NAME	DATE	AREA OF NEED

Be joyful in hope, patient in affliction, faithful in prayer.
— 1 John 5:14

TIMELINE	FOLLOW UP	OUTCOME

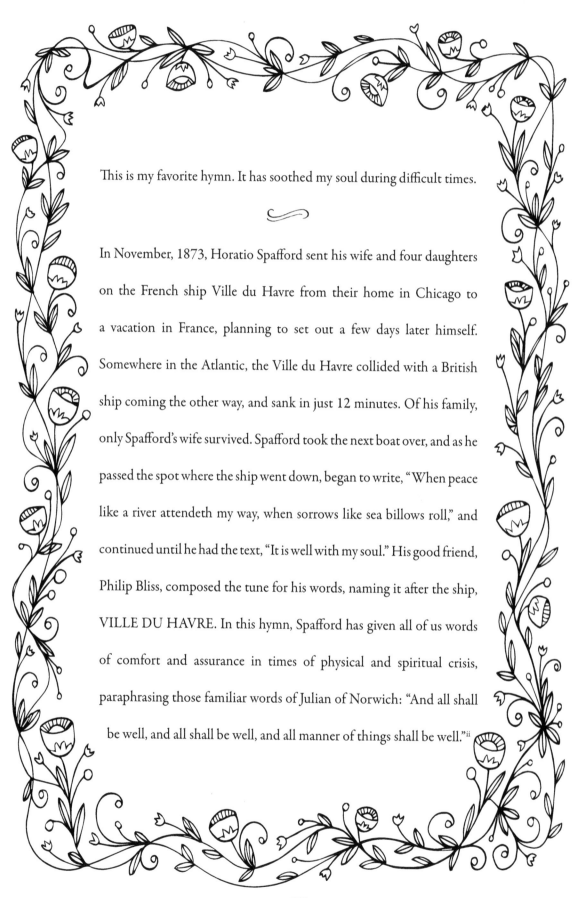

This is my favorite hymn. It has soothed my soul during difficult times.

In November, 1873, Horatio Spafford sent his wife and four daughters on the French ship Ville du Havre from their home in Chicago to a vacation in France, planning to set out a few days later himself. Somewhere in the Atlantic, the Ville du Havre collided with a British ship coming the other way, and sank in just 12 minutes. Of his family, only Spafford's wife survived. Spafford took the next boat over, and as he passed the spot where the ship went down, began to write, "When peace like a river attendeth my way, when sorrows like sea billows roll," and continued until he had the text, "It is well with my soul." His good friend, Philip Bliss, composed the tune for his words, naming it after the ship, VILLE DU HAVRE. In this hymn, Spafford has given all of us words of comfort and assurance in times of physical and spiritual crisis, paraphrasing those familiar words of Julian of Norwich: "And all shall be well, and all shall be well, and all manner of things shall be well."[ii]

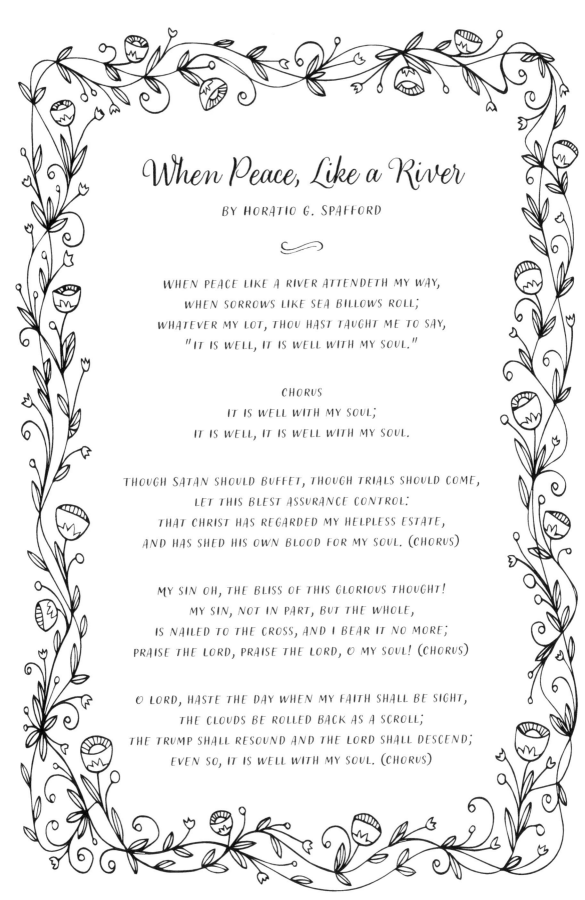

When Peace, Like a River

BY HORATIO G. SPAFFORD

WHEN PEACE LIKE A RIVER ATTENDETH MY WAY,
WHEN SORROWS LIKE SEA BILLOWS ROLL;
WHATEVER MY LOT, THOU HAST TAUGHT ME TO SAY,
"IT IS WELL, IT IS WELL WITH MY SOUL."

CHORUS
IT IS WELL WITH MY SOUL;
IT IS WELL, IT IS WELL WITH MY SOUL.

THOUGH SATAN SHOULD BUFFET, THOUGH TRIALS SHOULD COME,
LET THIS BLEST ASSURANCE CONTROL:
THAT CHRIST HAS REGARDED MY HELPLESS ESTATE,
AND HAS SHED HIS OWN BLOOD FOR MY SOUL. (CHORUS)

MY SIN OH, THE BLISS OF THIS GLORIOUS THOUGHT!
MY SIN, NOT IN PART, BUT THE WHOLE,
IS NAILED TO THE CROSS, AND I BEAR IT NO MORE;
PRAISE THE LORD, PRAISE THE LORD, O MY SOUL! (CHORUS)

O LORD, HASTE THE DAY WHEN MY FAITH SHALL BE SIGHT,
THE CLOUDS BE ROLLED BACK AS A SCROLL;
THE TRUMP SHALL RESOUND AND THE LORD SHALL DESCEND;
EVEN SO, IT IS WELL WITH MY SOUL. (CHORUS)

NOTES

Day 31 to 40: Prayer Is How We Ask For Help

i. Richards, Ramona. "Dirty Little Secret," *Today's Christian Woman*, May 5, 2007. http:www.christianitytoday.com/tcw/article_print.html?id=44838.

My Favorite Hymn

ii. https://hymnary.org/text/when_peace_like_a_river_attendeth_my_way

WAYS TO CONNECT

For more information, please visit Ruth's website, www.ruthhovsepian.com, where you will find her blog, speaking calendar, free resources, and all her latest news and information.

To book Ruth to speak at your next event, please visit ruthhovsepian.com or email info@ruthhovsepian.com for more details.

CPSIA information can be obtained
at www.ICGtesting.com
Printed in the USA
LVHW021415010622
720203LV00005B/57